More Than Conquerors

Worship
Resources
for Lent
and Easter

Gary Wayne Houston

C.S.S. Publishing Co., Inc.
Lima, Ohio

MORE THAN CONQUERORS

Copyright © 1989 by
The C.S.S. Publishing Company, Inc.
Lima, Ohio

You may copy the material in this publication if you are the original purchaser, for use as it was intended (worship material for worship use; educational material for classroom use; dramatic material for staging and production). No additional permission is required from the publisher for such copying by the original purchaser only. Inquiries should be addressed to: The C.S.S. Publishing Company, Inc., 628 South Main Street, Lima, Ohio 45804.

LIBRARY OF CONGRESS
Library of Congress Cataloging-in-Publication

Houston, Gary W., 1943-
    More than conquerors : worship resources for Lent and Easter / Gary Wayne Houston.
      p. cm.
    ISBN 1-556-73099-3
    1. Lent—Prayer-books and devotions—English. 2. Lenten sermons. 3. Easter service. 4. Easter—Sermons. 5. Sermons, American. 6. Liturgies.   I. Title.
BV85.H68   1989
264—dc19   88-24932
                                                                                   CIP

9810 / ISBN 1-55673-099-3   PRINTED IN U.S.A.

Table of Contents

Preface	5
Ash Wednesday and Lent	
Planning the Service	7
An Order of Service for Ash Wednesday	9
Scripture Resources on Repentance	14
Sermon: "What is Ash Wednesday and Lent?"	16
Sermon: "The Fear of God, the Blessing of God"	20
Palm Sunday	
Planning the Day	24
Invocation for Palm Sunday	26
Sermon: "Jesus and the Parade"	27
Maundy Thursday	
Candlelight Service for Maundy Thursday	32
Good Friday	
A Dramatic Reading	37
Sermon: "Father, Into Thy Hands"	43
Easter	
Planning for an Easter Vigil	46
An Easter Vigil Meditation	47
An Invocation for Easter Day	48
An Order of Service for Easter Day	49
Sermon: "The Easter Church"	52
Appendix: Hymn Resources	57
About the Author	58

*This book is dedicated to two
Logansport District Superintendents:*

The Rev. F. Kaye Bass

The Rev. Charles Johnson

*Thank you for your
love, prayers, and guidance.*

Preface

Worship can mean many things. For some it means prescribed rules and rubrics that must not be changed since they have been codified by the church. For us worship means what people do when they assemble together to praise God, receive the sacraments, and remember God's grace and forgiveness. People are divided, not only concerning what worship is, but in "how to do it." It is a significant issue for us because we sense that we *become* what we profess. How we pray determines how we develop in relationship with the Christ. For this reason we do not take worship lightly. Worship is what *people* do, although we are told in the Bible that the angels do it as well. Worship then, implies liturgy, which shapes the way we do things in church. We realize that worship is not only a private thing we do when we say our prayers. It includes also what we do when we come together as the mystical body of Christ, the church.

There can be good liturgy and bad liturgy. Good liturgy is not a spectator sport, but the work of the people. For this reason we use responsive readings, prayer in unison, calls to worship, and more. We do not go to church merely to "watch a show" or hear a sermon. We go to worship even if the meaning behind the experience may differ somewhat for each churchgoer. Good liturgy is not only orthodox in that it proclaims what has been everywhere and at all times taught. It is also balanced and does not ride a particular theological horse. Good liturgy invites the entire congregation in and does not exclude because of sex or race. Good liturgy reminds us that no one owns the church save Christ. It is his church and we are members or limbs of his organism.

Recently much has been made of liturgical renewal. We have seen new prayer books among some denominations and new hymnals among others. We have tried to speak to different needs, social and cultural situations. We have high church, low church, and free church. We can live with the options, but we cannot live without the church. We need the church not only as a place to praise God, but a place to find nourishment as well. People come to church for one basic reason (aside from loyalty): they come to find hope. This is why so many speak such things as "I don't get anything out of it anymore." When they speak so, they are describing the condition of their souls, but we who are pastors have been given a "cure of souls." We must not forget this. What we recommend is liturgy that speaks to and for the people of the local congregation. It is not useful to insist that a small country congregation use a cantor and holy water if that is not their custom. We who are pastors not only represent, in a real way, God to our people; we also represent our people to God. Sometime we will be called to account and neither process theology, ecumenism, nor Paul Tillich will be there to help us. Only Christ will be there, just as he is with us now in our worship and in our preaching.

This book is designed to provide some resources and ideas that can be used to further the preaching of Christ. Please take what is useful and ignore the rest. Feel free to use these ideas, just as I have used the ideas of many others before me.

There was within me a real struggle as to whether or not to write a Holy Communion service for Easter. I chose not. Among those in the denomination I serve, few celebrate Holy Communion on Easter. Perhaps the reason is that we celebrate Maundy Thursday only a few days before. Another more practical reason is that the Easter crowds are large and many of us want to focus on other things. One such focus is baptism. Easter has always been the traditional day of baptism and entry into the church. There is no stronger witness than that of baptizing a few dozen people on this day. I always confirm the children on Easter and baptize as many as will stand still long enough. The white of Easter not only stands for the purity of Christ, it also reminds us of the robes we shall all wear in heaven.

All of us are thankful that others have spiritually formed us. Many have helped to shape my life. I remember many, many preachers that "ran around with" my father, a Christian church minister for thirty some years. Urban T. Holmes very much influenced me although I make no claims to his theological expertise. In the United Methodist structure I had two District Superintendents who did all they could to keep me out of trouble during the first few years of my ministry: F. Kaye Bass and Charles ("Chuck") Johnson. This book can be seen as appreciation to them, but they are not responsible for its content. And, finally, there was "Father Bob," the Rev. Robert Anderson of Bedford, Indiana. He sped me on my way to seminary. To these, to my wife Joyce, and to my children who have loved me and prayed both for and with me, I say thank you. My mother, Margie (Murphy) Houston, has prayed probably more than any other mother since Saint Augustine's mother Monica. May we all meet someday in that heaven we profess.

The Bible translation used in this worship resource is the New International Version.

Planning for Ash Wednesday

Many Protestant denominations are begging to experience the rich symbolism connected with Lent. Especially new for many is the imposition of ashes. Many of us ignore — or even miss — Lent, giving it no more notice than perhaps to add a Bible study to the church calendar. Many of us clergy are more focused on Easter and big crowds than we are on Lent or something as old-fashioned as Ash Wednesday.

In the local congregation where I presently serve we recently shared what we called a Sacrificial Meal. This was done to symbolize "giving up something for Lent." We had potato soup. We served only water to drink. We did not even have coffee. This did not make some of the younger people happy. They expected cola. At this meal we read Psalms, followed by a quiet time for reflection and prayer.

People were asked to write down some particular bad habit, private sin, or anything which held them back from total surrender to Jesus Christ. Then we placed the papers in a large metal pan and burned them. We concluded with a joyful song and benediction. You might try this, or some variation of this in your congregation.

In the unlikely event that you do not know, ashes can be purchased from any Christian supply house such as Cokesbury. *Do not* use ashes from a fireplace or any such source. The impurities in the ashes could irritate the skin. It is an honored tradition among some groups to save palms from one year's Palm Sunday celebration and to burn them for use on Ash Wednesday the year following.

The pastor, or the one imposing the ashes (and I recommend the pastor), will want to have a damp towel nearby for cleansing the hands after the imposition is completed.

The ashes can be put in any kind of small bowl, but pewter or silver is more traditional. You can use a chalice if you like. A new set of meanings is communicated when you do this.

You might instruct the people from the pulpit and in your parish newsletter several weeks before Ash Wednesday. If the service is new to them you can expect low participation unless you stress for them the importance of this service. In my own experience I have had one-fifth (or less) of my average Sunday morning worship attendance at any evening Ash Wednesday service. You can, of course, combine the imposition of ashes with a Sunday service, but that breaks the whole tradition of Ash *Wednesday.*

The observance of Ash Wednesday goes a long way in raising people's consciousness of what Lent is all about. It is prophetic in that it gives a sign instead of only giving a sermon or teaching. It *shows* what is meant.

If you would like more information, there are many reference books available. The best single resource of a non-technical nature is *From Ashes to Fire* (Nashville: Abingdon, 1979). C.S.S. Publishing has several worship resources, several of which have excellent introductions.

Introduction to the Ash Wednesday Service

The first part of this service is based on "The Firste Daie Of Lent" found in *The First and Second Prayer Books of King Edward VI*. While there is no copyright on this old service, it has been included in a book with the same title (Dent: London, Everyman's Library, 1968), pp. 280-85. There is an introduction to this book by Douglas Harrison. I have extensively modernized and altered the text. The Bible translation used for the Curses is the NIV. The Thanksgiving over the Ashes is adapted from *A Manual For Priests of the American Church*, (Cambridge: Society of Saint John the Evangelist, 1970), p. 221. Again, I have extensively modified the language used.

The First Day of Lent
Commonly Called
Ash Wednesday

(The people being called together by the ringing of a bell and assembled in the church, the litany shall be said in the accustomed manner. The minister goes to the pulpit and says:)

Admonition

Brothers and sisters in Christ, in the early days of the church there was a godly discipline at the beginning of Lent for notorious sinners. They were put to open penitence, and punished in this world, that their souls might be saved. All of us have been or are notorious sinners. These sinners were admonished so that by their example others would be more hesitant to offend God. After this punishment the offenders were restored to the church body. Let us follow today in this ancient practice and apply to ourselves this Ash Wednesday the curses against sin found in Deuteronomy 27.

After each sentence please answer "Amen." By this you will be called to earnest and true repentance and may walk more aware of the days found in the ways of the world. Even if you think these curses do not apply to things you have done, trust that God's Holy Word applies to all people everywhere. You and I are accountable to God for our deeds. We can substitute in our thinking and prayers our own sins instead of those read. Know that a Holy God loves sinners who repent, but despises sin.

Minister: Cursed is the man who carves an image or casts an idol — a thing detestable to the LORD, the work of the craftsman's hands — and sets it up in secret.
People: **Amen!**
Minister: Cursed is the man who dishonors his father or his mother.
People: **Amen!**
Minister: Cursed is the man who moves his neighbor's boundary stone.
People: **Amen!**
Minister: Cursed is the man who leads the blind astray on the road.
People: **Amen!**
Minister: Cursed is the man who withholds justice from the alien, the fatherless or the widow.
People: **Amen!**
Minister: Cursed is the man who sleeps with his father's wife, for he dishonors his father's bed.
People: **Amen!**
Minister: Cursed is the man who has sexual relations with any animal.
People: **Amen!**
Minister: Cursed is the man who sleeps with his sister, the daughter of his father or the daughter of his mother.
People: **Amen!**
Minister: Cursed is the man who sleeps with his mother-in-law.

People: **Amen!**
Minister: Cursed is the man who kills his neighbor secretly.
People: **Amen!**
Minister: Cursed is the man who accepts a bribe to kill an innocent person.
People: **Amen!**
Minister: Cursed is the man who does not uphold the words of this law by carrying them out.
People: **Amen!**
Minister: Now hear these additional curses from the One Holy God. Cursed is the one who puts their trust in other people and departs from trust in God.
People: **Amen!**
Minister: Cursed are the unforgiving, the fornicators and adulterers, those who desire what others have, and who practice self-righteousness.
People: **Amen!**
Minister: Now seeing that all who do these things are cut off from God unless they ask forgiveness (as the Prophet David bears witness), let us remember the judgment hanging over our heads and return to our Lord God. Let us do this with humbleness of heart, acknowledging our sins, confessing our offences, and seeking from now on to bring forth worthy fruits of penitence.
People: **For even now is the axe put to the root of the tree. Every tree that does not bring forth good fruit is hewn down and cast into the fire. It is truly a fearful thing to fall into the hands of the living God. God will rain down snares, fire, brimstone, storm and tempest upon unrepentant sinners.**
Minister: For the Lord is coming from heaven to judge the wickedness of sinners. Who may stand in the day of the Lord's coming? The Lord will gather the wheat into the barn, but burn the chaff with unquenchable fire.

People: **The day of the Lord comes as a thief in the night when all are saying "Peace." Then shall the day of destruction come upon them as the sorrow that comes upon a woman during childbirth. They shall not escape.**

Minister: God continually calls sinners to repentance. But in that day when they call upon God there will be no answer. God has said that then they shall not find me. They have hated knowledge and have not received the fear of the Lord.

People: **They have despised the correction of God. At that time it will be too late to knock for the door will be shut. It is too late to cry for mercy when it is the time for justice.**

Minister: Let us not abuse the goodness of God, who mercifully calls us to amend our ways. Out of God's endless pity we are promised forgiveness of what is past. Let us turn loose of our past and turn to a future in Christ.

Lessons and Proclamation

Hymn: "Are Ye Able?"

First Reading: Zechariah 7:4-10

(A period of silence may be observed)

Second Reading: 1 Corinthians 9:19-27

Hymn: "How Great Thou Art"

Holy Gospel: Luke 5:29-35

The Sermon or Meditation

Thanksgiving Over the Ashes

Minister: O God, who desires not the death of a sinner, but rather that he or she should turn from sin and be saved: mercifully look down upon the frailty of our mortal nature. Of your goodness bless these ashes now to be set upon our heads in token of humility and to obtain your pardon.
We acknowledge that we are but dust, and that for our unworthiness, unto dust shall we return. May we through your mercy be found ready to receive forgiveness of all our sins, and those good things which you have promised to the penitent. Through Christ our Lord. Amen

Repentance

Penitents file forward and kneel or stand. Ashes are applied to the forehead of each penitent who is at the front. The minister may make the sign of the cross on their forehead with the ashes saying: "Repent and believe the good news of salvation!"

Reconciliation

Minister: In the name of Jesus Christ you are forgiven!

People: **In the name of Jesus Christ you are forgiven!**

The Lord's Prayer

Hymn: "On a Hill Far Away"

Dismissal

Minister: Go forth rejoicing in your future in Jesus Christ!

People: **Amen and Amen Forever!**

Scripture Resources on Repentance

Any of the following Scriptures can be utilized in responsive readings, calls to worship, or dramatic readings during the season of Lent:

Old Testament

Leviticus 26:40-42	Psalm 130	Jeremiah 26:3, 13
Deuteronomy 4:29-31	Isaiah 31:6	Jeremiah 36:3-7
Deuteronomy 30:1	Isaiah 44:22	Ezekiel 7:16-20
1 Kings 8:33-50	Isaiah 55:6,7	Ezekiel 16:61-63
2 Chronicles 7:14	Isaiah 57:15	Ezekiel 18:21-31
2 Chronicles 30:6-9	Isaiah 59:20	Ezekiel 33:10-13
Nehemiah 1:9	Isaiah 61:1,2	Ezekiel 37:23
Job 11:13-15	Jeremiah 3:4-19	Hosea 10:12
Job 22:23	Jeremiah 4:1-14	Hosea 12:6
Job 33:26-28	Jeremiah 6:8	Hosea 14:1-2
Psalm 22	Jeremiah 7:5-7	Joel 2:12-18
Psalm 51	Jeremiah 13:15, 16	Amos 5:6
	Jeremiah 24:7	Haggai 1:7

New Testament

Matthew 3:2-8	Luke 24:47	2 Timothy 2:25
Matthew 9:13	Acts 2:38	Hebrews 6:1
Mark 6:12	Acts 3:19	James 4:8-10
Luke 5:32	Acts 8:22	1 John 1:9
Luke 13:1-5	Acts 26:20	Revelation 2:5
Luke 15:7	Romans 2:4	Revelation 3:2-19
Luke 18:13, 14	Romans 14:11	

Consider now these promises to all who repent:

Old Testament

Leviticus 26:40-42	Psalm 6:8	Psalm 34:18
Deuteronomy 4:29-31	Psalm 9:10	Psalm 145:18, 19
Deuteronomy 30:1-10	Psalm 22:26	Ezekiel 18:21-23
Job 33:26-28	Psalm 24:3	

New Testament

Matthew 5:4
Matthew 6:14
Matthew 7:7-11
Matthew 12:20-31

Luke 6:37
Luke 15:4-32
Luke 18:10-14
John 6:37

John 10:9
Acts 13:38
Romans 10:9-13
1 John 1:9

What is Ash Wednesday and Lent?

A Meditation

Ash Wednesday is the first day of the season of Lent. The word "Lent" in English really means "Spring." Therefore, we should easily be able to remember that this season preceeds Easter. In fact, Ash Wednesday comes six and one-half weeks before Easter Sunday.

There are forty *weekdays* to the season of Lent. This symbolizes the forty-day fasts of Moses, Elijah and Jesus. All three of these persons fasted for the same period of time. Although "forty" might have had a symbolic meaning to those writing the Bible, it was later taken literally. Be that as it may, the tradition of both Ash Wednesday and Lent goes back to the early church.

What is special about Ash Wednesday? What do the ashes mean and why are they used? They mean two things:

1. They are symbolic of *purification*. We are given this in Numbers 19:17 and following, and in Hebrews 9:13.

2. They are symbolic of the *repentance* that a sinner needs before a just God. Clear examples of this meaning are given especially in Jonah 3:6, Luke 10:13, and Matthew 11:21.

We know that the entire Christian congregation began receiving the imposition of ashes from at least the tenth century. At first the ashes were mixed with water and then the bishop sprinkled this solution upon the congregation. Later it became more common only to use the ashes and to make the sign of the cross on the forehead of all those who wished to publically show repentance, especially for the sins of the previous year.

By the imposition of ashes, Christians were and are reminded of their humility before the one, holy God. We are to remember that we were made out of the dust and that we shall return to that same dust. The imposition of ashes is a sign of God's grace for all the penitent. This service belongs to the church universal.

Ashes remind us of death and resurrection. We know that our bodies will turn to ashes in the grave, but we look forward in faith to the resurrection in that last day when we will be given new bodies in Christ. We will be bodily raised to dwell with him in new, glorified bodies. We do not know, any more than did the Apostle Paul, what these bodies will be like. We accept this mystery in faith.

At the Committal of the Dead the priest or minister says something like the following to those who are present and as a blessing over the deceased:

> *In sure and certain hope of the resurrection to eternal life through our Lord Jesus Christ, we commend to Almighty God our* brother, N.; *and we commit* his *body to the ground; earth to earth, ashes to ashes, dust to dust. The Lord bless* him *and keep* him, *the Lord make his face to shine upon* him *and be gracious unto* him, *the Lord lift up his countenance upon* him *and give* him *peace. Amen.*
> (*Book of Common Prayer*, p. 485.)

Ashes remind us that God has made us from the earth and that we therefore have a relationship to all creation. We are reminded that our very bodies are meant to glorify our Creator as we act as caretakers of this world for God.

The imposition of ashes does not have as its object to make us feel guilty over what we have done. Rather it is meant to lead us to repentance and change. The ashes bid us to become better persons in Christ. Every Ash Wednesday we are given a chance to start all over again, much as we do with New Year's resolutions. Out of the ashes of our past sins rise new creatures.

Briefly we turn now to Lent. What is Lent? Lent was originally a time of preparation of candidates for baptism on Easter Sunday. These candidates prepared during the forty days of Lent for this initiation into Christian life.

Lent had to do, then, with *preparation*. It was and is a time to get ready for God to make a change in our lives.

Lent soon added another meaning to preparation. It became that one, special season during which those who had been alienated and lapsed from the church could be *reconciled* and *restored* to Christian fellowship through prayer and penance. In the early church a lapsed member needed to visibly show that he or she repented of sinful actions. One repented and was forgiven. It is still that way with Christians.

Besides being a time of preparation and a time of repentance for all believers, Lent also became associated with things such as self-denial, intensive Bible study, increased time in prayer, sacrificial giving of money to the church and sincere fellowship with other Christian believers. In short, Lent became a time for renewal both within the church and in the lives of individual believers.

Lent, in addition to all this, is a time for evangelism and true conversion to the Christian faith. It is a season for growing in Christian maturity. Lent is that special season that calls us to *service*. It beckons us toward the basin and towel of Maundy Thursday.

Lent is not merely "giving up something." It is a time to take upon ourselves the intention of becoming serious about being a Christian. It symbolizes true participation in the mystery of God-with-us!

Lent also gets us ready for the Easter season and the joy associated with it. Lent is a time of self-examination, not morbid introspection. It is a time for self-appraisal and of new beginnings.

The color for Lent is purple. This is a symbol of our embarrassment before God. We blush as we recall our many sins and wrong doings. This color turns to white with Easter. This is a reminder that, once we sincerely confess from the bottom of our hearts, we are created anew under the power of God. Lent represents repentance. Easter represents resurrection. Between these two, stands the cross of Good Friday, which represents forgiveness.

It is not enough to feel bad about our sins. Rather we should, with the help of Jesus Christ, give them up. We strive for holiness under the atoning power of the Cross. Lent, like the Spring, is a time for renewal and can prompt the beginning buds of spiritual flowers. These flowers blossom at Easter.

To conclude, Lent is the most serious season of the church year. But it is a wonderful and glorious church season. It is that time which prepares us for Holy Week. May we all pray, study, and nourish one another this Lent. May we grow in love and faith as we look forward with eagerness to Easter.

The Fear of God, The Blessing of God

A Lenten Meditation
Psalm 128

Dag Hammarskjold, former Secretary-General of the United Nations, wrote of "the chaos you become without God's hand," and of the chaos of the world caused by this chaos in ourselves.

W. B. Yeats declared in his "Second Coming":

Things fall apart; the center cannot hold, mere anarchy is loosed upon the world.

Both writers declare what is happening in our world today. We live in a world that is seen by many as meaningless. We need only recall the plays by Sartre ("No Exit"), and Beckett ("Waiting For Godot"). Or we can read Camus, Rilke, or Dostoevski and see that this meaninglessness has been felt for some time now in literature.

The Christian realizes that without the fear of God (some call it "awe"), the world truly falls apart. God acts as a structuring device, One who allows us to put things and thoughts into a system. We know who we are because we are related to God. And we see others in relationship to Jesus Christ. Proverbs 1:7 reminds us that the beginning of wisdom is fear of the Lord. In our hurry to acknowledge the love of God we forget this sense of awe and fear that we can have toward the One who made us. Maybe some of this comes from the strange American custom of democratizing everything and everyone. We are in a hurry to call people by their first name after we have only met them once. For many of us, God is no exception.

Psalm 128 reminds us that a holy awe toward God is necessary for our spiritual being. Let us look at this Psalm as having three major lessons for us:

1. Blessings are a result of a life lived in holiness.
2. A blessed and holy life is a life that is dedicated to hard work.
3. The real joys of life come only as a result of love and fear toward God. As a result of this, we experience personal and domestic peace.

1. *First of all, we need to live holy lives.* The basic building block of a holy life is fear of God. Proverbs 19:23 reads:

The fear of the LORD leads to
  life:
Then one rests content,
  untouched by trouble.

It is important to realize that we do not speak here of magical thinking. We do not act a certain way and compel God to do such and so. Nor does the fear of God mean some kind of dread or guilty feeling when you enter a church. Rather, the fear of God has to do with the respect and acknowledgment of his holiness.

Since everything we are or have depends upon God, there is no meaning to our lives apart from God. When we fail to worship the Creator and worship the creature instead, we wind up alienated from our center. We become off balance. An easy way to check this out is to look at those who live for the pleasure of the moment in drugs, wealth, parties, and the like.

When our very center is empty we will never be able to fill it up with wine, women and song. New clothes wear out. False friends fall away. The so-called god of pleasure is a Satan that always lets its worshipers down. The Living God never fails us.

T. L. Metcalfe once said, "God's blessings are continually falling. If we want them to fall on us we must be where they are falling. They are falling thickest near his throne. Therefore, the closer to God we get, the more blessings we receive." Psalm 128 teaches us that the fear of God allows us access to his throne. Fearing God is another way of obeying God. Fear leads to obedience.

Hebrews 5:7 reminds us: "During the days of Jesus' life on earth, he offered up prayers and petitions with loud cries and tears to the one who could save him from death, and he was heard because of his reverent submission." Are you and I known for the godly fear that we have? Do people around us even know that we are Christians?

Perhaps the greatest reward God could ever give any of us is peace of mind and contentment. Listen to these words of David, as recorded in 2 Samuel 23:2-4:

The Spirit of the LORD
   spoke through me;
his word was on my
   tongue.
The God of Israel spoke,
the Rock of Israel said to
   me:
"When one rules over men in
   righteousness,
when he rules in the fear of God,
he is like the light of morning
   at sunrise
on a cloudless morning,
like the brightness after rain
that brings the grass from
   the earth."

2. *Secondly, a blessed and holy life requires that we earn a livelihood.* We would think this so obvious that it would not need mentioning. Verse 2 of Psalm 128 says, "You will eat the fruit of your labor; blessings and prosperity will be yours." This is quite a promise when you stop and reflect.

Religion teaches that work gives us dignity. God wants us to work. All of us may not work with our hands, but the more idle we become the more we fall into that stance mentioned earlier. The very idle lack purpose and meaning to life. Since I am a United Methodist I am not afraid to remind us that the early Methodists were known as those who loved God, worked hard and were thrifty with their money. This does not mean they were stingy with the Lord's portion. They were not.

This, then, is appropriate counsel if you are unhappy: get busy and do something! Make something! Build something! Create something! If you do this you will be happier. We do not condemn or judge those out of work, but no one need lie around and be bored. God has given us an exciting world to discover and few of us know all the gifts and talents with which God has endowed us. We speak too much of talent and too little of the work needed to develop that talent.

3. *Thirdly, and finally, the real joys of life are a result of the love and fear that we acknowledge for God.* As a result of our fear of the Lord we are granted personal and domestic peace. We do not need to know how it works. But it does! And it is not bad theology to say so.

Hear these verses of Psalm 128: "You will eat the fruit of your labor; blessings and prosperity will be yours. Your wife will be like a fruitful vine within your house; your sons will be like olive shoots around your table. Thus is the man blessed who fears the LORD." Now God grants blessings to women in the same way. They are not excluded. But what is important here is to realize that the basis for a happy home is built upon fear of God.

Sometimes we are so sophisticated that we do not master the basics. Too easily we put ourselves first, in position ahead of God, and often we do not even realize that this has happened. Fear of God is basic.

Psalm 128 closes in an optimistic manner. All of us wish our lives would close in the same way. But the Lord has been good to us already. Maybe some of us have never noticed. This is why we had this brief Lenten meditation on the fear of God. We need to see what we already have, and leave the rest to God's good graces.

Planning for Palm Sunday

The joy and festivity of this day can hardly be surpassed (although John Wesley particularly enjoyed All Saints' Day). There are many ways to enhance the service on this day. Here are two which have worked in local churches where I have served.

The first thing that worked well was to use banners on this day. We had every Sunday church school class design and make their own banner. This was to witness to that first Palm Sunday as a "parade," but also to lift up our Sunday church school program. In all, there were eight banners used (but you could have banners for the women's groups and the men's groups as well). The procession of banners began in the back of the worship area. We entered with triumphant music.

We had prepared string (several thicknesses) at each window that lined the sides of the sanctuary. At the end of each string we put a strong paper clip. The banners were placed there and at one special command from the Sunday church school superintendent these banners were hoisted up the wall to the middle of the windows. This created a dramatic effect, much like unfurling the American flag during the singing of the Star-Spangled Banner.

This idea worked well. Everyone enjoys seeing little children involved and we included several dozen in the parade. At the head of the procession of banners was a boy who carried the cross. We had him carry it high, in a ceremonial manner. If you have individuals in your congregation who march with a school band, they can share hints (as can a good baton twirler). The people, who were singing, were waving their palm branches all the while.

A second idea that we have used in a congregation is to have the entire congregation walk along and sing while waving palms. We walked down the hall of the Christian education wing and back to the sanctuary. From time to time someone would shout: "Hosanna!" Many people who might have thought this silly seemed to enjoy it once they became involved. As we came back into the sanctuary we all exchanged the peace and became better acquainted with people we did not know well. We allowed about fifteen minutes for the parade and the handshaking. Then the choir began a joyful tune and everyone knew it was time to sit down. Even the children seemed more relaxed, having gotten so much movement out of their systems.

If the weather permits, the parade can be held outdoors. Whatever you do on Palm Sunday, let it glorify Christ. Nothing says you cannot — or should not — have fun doing this.

Invocation for Palm Sunday

O God, the maker of us all, look down upon us today and see our joy. Father, we celebrate this day the triumph of your Son as he entered Jerusalem riding on the symbol of peace, the lowly donkey. Like those who watched him ride in so many years ago, we also wave our palms and shout Hosanna. Remind us of that element of celebration that we so often lack in our lives. Renew us with joy as we shout out, affirming you in our lives. Release us from the burdens of the sins that we all secretly carry. Forgive us and sustain us as we worship in your house today. Amen

Jesus and the Parade

A Sermon for Palm Sunday
Mark 11:1-10

All of us like the excitement of parades. We have every reason to suppose the people of Jerusalem in Jesus' day liked them as well.

The time of the Jewish Passover was a national holiday. On this first Palm Sunday we can almost see the priests in the temple courtyard, the merchants hawking their wares, the noisy crowds of pilgrims who have streamed into the big city from the countryside, and the children as they laugh and play in the narrow streets. It was a festive time. It was fun to celebrate the Jewish festivals and to step out of the everyday humdrum of work. It was a divine pause in life.

Into the holy city of Jerusalem rode a new kind of king that day. He was on a donkey — not even a white charger, but a donkey! Why a donkey? According to various Bible commentators, the donkey had a special meaning. When a king entered into a city riding on a donkey it meant that he had come in peace. If he rode in on a horse it meant war.

Jesus had come in peace to usher in the first phase of a new kingdom. He was demonstrating with this symbolic action what he was and is all about. He acted as a prophet with a "sign of peace." This is what the donkey represented. It represented peace and new beginnings.

G. K. Chesterton wrote a poem about that donkey. He said:

When fishes flew and forests walk'd
  And figs grew upon thorn.
Some moment when the moon was blood
  Then surely I was born.

With monstrous head and sickening cry
  And ears like errant wings,
The devil's walking parody
  Of all four-footed things.

> *The tatter'd outlaw of the earth*
> *Of ancient crooked will;*
> *Starve, scourge, deride me, I am dumb,*
> *I keep my secret still.*
>
> *Fools! For I also had my hour,*
> *One far fierce hour and sweet;*
> *There was a shout about my ears,*
> *And palms before my feet.*

So much for donkeys. Let us now consider the palms used on that first Palm Sunday. What do the palms mean? We associate palms with Palm Sunday just as we associate a Christmas tree with Christmas. But why palms?

There were sacred associations with the palm tree throughout the ancient Near East. This tree often appeared on cylinder seals and in other art forms. It was carved in relief on the walls, doors and generally used as decoration in Solomon's Temple, according to 1 Kings. Similar decorations have been found in Assyrian temples and other royal buildings.

Palm Sunday, of course, received its name from the use of palm branches when Jesus entered Jerusalem, a day we celebrate as the beginning of Holy Week. But there is another biblical reference to palms and worship in Scripture. Revelation 7:9 describes the white-robed multitude standing before God's throne. They hold palm branches as they sing their praises.

A third element of this first Palm Sunday parade was the crowd. Every parade must have a crowd. It is not hard to visualize thousands of people cheering and putting down palm branches on that day. John Scotford wrote a Palm Sunday sermon in 1955 that distinguished between two types of people in the crowd that day: *applauders* and *plodders*. The plodders were the faithful band of disciples and friends that had followed Jesus all over the country throughout his ministry.

The plodders had hung in there out of sheer loyalty to the person of Jesus. They followed him even when they sometimes misunderstood him. Scotford describes them as follows:

> *Plodding along in the center of the picture was a small company of country folk. Their clothes were both dated and dusty. They spoke a Galilean accent. They approached Jerusalem and its people with timidity, fearing lest they be made sport of. Only when they looked toward Jesus did a gleam of confident determination appear in their eyes. He was their hope and their stay. It was because of him that they were there. Blind loyalty rather than intelligent reasoning had brought them on this fool's journey to Jerusalem. (Scotford, p. 37.)*

The plodders were the faithful, rag-tag group that hung in there through the hard days and through the good days. But notice one thing: they kept their eyes on Jesus and followed him without question.

The other group at the parade was the applauders. They had heard about this Galilean prophet who claimed to be the Messiah, who claimed to be the Son of God. The people wanted to take a look at such a person.

There is no reason to judge these applauders as bad people! They were drawn to Jesus because they were curious, but they also wanted some hope for living. Perhaps he was the one. They asked themselves and each other: Who was this man riding into town on a donkey? Who was this Jesus who claimed to be a Jewish king? But, as Scotford wisely points out, they "betokened encouragement rather than support."

Nearly every local church has its share of plodders and applauders. The plodders serve on committees, attend church regularly, contribute as much money as they can and keep their eyes on Jesus as best they know how. The applauders are more likely to show up that first Sunday to greet a new pastor or to come for a special event. Although all this may be true, it is better to be an applauder than someone who is totally disinterested in Jesus and his parade. Applauders know that they want to be included among the faithful, but they lack energy or faith.

Whether we are plodders or applauders, however, we must

not forget that the excitement of the parade on Sunday was followed by the Cross on Friday. The crowd that had shouted "Hosanna!" on Sunday shouted "Crucify him!" on Friday. We dare not think we would have done differently. There is a powerful element to group dynamics. The power of the mob has been responsible for damaging or destroying many churches and lives.

And, although the church has become more and more a celebration body in the twentieth century, we must not forget the Cross. The Cross is what Jesus and the parade was all about. Between Palm Sunday and its wonderful celebration and Easter Sunday and its celebration falls the shadow of the Cross. The church exists not only to nuture its members, but to spread the Good News of the Cross. Without the Cross, Palm Sunday makes no sense.

We have a story to tell. The parade led to Calvary and to forgiveness. That is very good news! And maybe the best way to close this meditation is to quote a poem that speaks of that Cross so very well. It is entitled "There Is a Man on the Cross," and was written by Elizabeth Cheney:

> *When there is silence around me*
> *By day or by night —*
> *I am startled by a cry.*
> *It came down from the cross —*
> *The first time I heard it.*
> *I went out and searched —*
> *And found a man in the throes of crucifixion,*
> *And I said, "I will take you down,"*
> *And I tried to take the nails out of His feet.*
> *But He said, "Let them be*
> *For I cannot be taken down*
> *Until every man, every woman, and every child*
> *Come together to take me down."*
> *And I said, "But I cannot hear you cry.*
> *What can I do?"*
> *And He said, "Go about the world —*
> *Tell everyone that you meet —*
> *There is a man on the cross."*

Notes

William Barclay, *The Gospel of Mark: Daily Study Bible Series*, (Philadelphia: The Westminster Press, 1975), p. 264.

John Scotford, "Applauders or Plodders?", *Pulpit Digest*, 35: March 1955, number 203, pp. 37-40.

Elizabeth Cheney, "There Is a Man On The Cross," *Baker's Pocket Treasury of Religious Verse*, compiled by Donald T. Kauffman, (Grand Rapids: Baker Book House, 1962), p. 143.

A Candlelight Service
For Maundy Thursday

Prelude What Wondrous Love Is This
(or: Alas! And Did My Savior Bleed)

Meditation

What exactly does this night mean to us? Why are we gathered here? All of us must answer this question for ourselves. All of us must go into that Upper Room for ourselves. It is not enough to accept the belief structure of our parents. It is not enough to accept Jesus because it seems nice. No. We must enter into the quiet of our hearts and say: "Lord, I am here because I love you." That can be a powerful reason for being here. Pray that all discover this love for Christ.

The six candles that stand lit on the altar represent unity of faith

Call to Worship

Liturgist: Let us remember that first Holy Communion Service.
People: **We are here to remember the One who not only sat at table, but who also had the basin and towel.**
Liturgist: Remembering means re-creating once more the meaning of that night. We experience Christ here.
People: **Let us break bread together.**

Hymn: "My Faith Look Up to Thee"

Prayer of Confession (in unison)

Almighty God, Creator of all that is, be present in our hearts this night. Renew our faith and stir us to new service. Remind us of our Lord's call to each of us. Let us stand united tonight in the faith. Let us put aside any differences and accept one another as brothers and sisters in Christ.

*The first light reminds us of Judas —
the Judas in all of us.*

Liturgist: When evening came, Jesus was reclining at the table with the Twelve. And while they were eating, he said, "I tell you the truth, one of you will betray me."

People: **They were very sad and began to say to him one after the other, "Surely not I, Lord?"**

Liturgist: Jesus replied, "The one who has dipped his hand into the bowl with me will betray me."

People: **Then Judas, the one who would betray him, said, "Surely not I, Rabbi?"**

The First Light is Extinguished

Choral Anthem

*The second light reminds us of
darkness which is in us all.*

Liturgist: Jesus went as usual to the Mount of Olives, and his disciples followed him. On reaching the place, he said to them, "Pray that you will not fall into temptation."

People: **Father, if you are willing, take this cup from me; yet not my will, but yours be done.**

Liturgist: When he rose from prayer and went back to the disciples, he found them asleep.

People: **Why are you sleeping? Get up and pray so that you will not fall into temptation.**

Liturgist: And it was very dark all around them.

Hymn: " 'Tis Midnight, and on Olive's Brow"

Words of Comfort

Pastor: Even in the darkest night God is with us. Even when we fall asleep in our temptation time the Lord is near.
People: **Let us hear his voice. We are his sheep.**

The Second Light is Extinguished

> *The third light reminds*
> *us of our disunity.*

Prayer for Forgiveness

(May be said by Pastor or by People in unison)

We remember this night that we are not united. We repent of our power struggles and our perversion of the church. We realize that we put ourselves first over others and that we do not recognize others as Christ. On this night as we sit here in a comfortable church there are others who would like to be here. But because they were old, or handicapped, we found them too much trouble to bring along.

Lord, reunite us. Help us heal old hurts and old memories. Reconcile us to each other to our parents, and to our children. Let us sit at table with you, united in you. May we realize that what we have in common with one another is you. Forgive us our disunity, Lord.

Liturgist: While they were eating, Jesus took bread, gave thanks and broke it, and gave it to his disciples, saying, "Take and eat; this is my body."

People: **Then he took the cup, gave thanks and offered it to them, saying, "Drink from it, all of you. This is the blood of the covenant, which is poured out for many of the forgiveness of sins."**

The Third Light is Extinguished

(Open Communion, with persons coming and going as they desire. When all desiring have come, the service continues)

Hymn: "Break Thou The Bread Of Life"

*The fourth light
reminds us of pride.*

Liturgist: At that time the disciples came to Jesus and asked, "Who is greatest in the kingdom of heaven?"
People: **He called a little child and had him stand among them.**
Liturgist: And he said: "I tell you the truth, unless you change and become like little children, you will never enter the kingdom of heaven.
People: **Therefore, whoever humbles himself like this child is the greatest in the kingdom of heaven."**

Special Music

The Fourth Light is Extinguished

*The fifth light
reminds us of service.*

Minister or Liturgist: So he got up from the meal, took off his outer clothing, and wrapped a towel around his waist.
People: **After that, he poured water into a basin and began to wash his disciples' feet, drying them with the towel that was wrapped around him.**

Minister or Liturgist: He came to Simon Peter, who said to him, "Lord, are you going to wash my feet?"

People: **Jesus replied, "You do not realize now what I am doing, but later you will understand."**

Minister or Liturgist: "No," said Peter, "you shall never wash my feet."

People: **Jesus answered, "Unless I wash you, you have no part with me."**

Minister or Liturgist: "Then, Lord," Simon Peter replied, "not just my feet but my hands and my head as well!"

Hymn: "Let All Mortal Flesh Keep Silence"

The Fifth Light is Extinguished

The sixth light, which remains burning, signifies Christ as the light of the world.

Pastor: This last light reminds us that it is never entirely dark for the one who follows Christ. You and I leave this place having sat at table with our Lord. It is now time to rise up from this meal and to serve him. May we all look forward to having the heavenly banquet with our Lord in heaven. And may he bless each one of us to his service. Amen

The people leave in silence

A Dramatic Reading For Good Friday

Before the Cross

First Reader: He then began to teach them that the Son of Man must suffer many things and be rejected by the elders, chief priests and teachers of the law, and that he must be killed and after three days rise again. He spoke plainly about this, and Peter took him aside and began to rebuke him.

Second Reader: We never really believe him, do we? Even when he told us that he was going to die — even then we called him wrong.

Third Reader: Can you imagine Peter rebuking our Lord? I'm glad I've never done anything like that. Lord, I would *never* betray you.

Jesus: I tell you the truth. Today — yes, tonight — before the rooster crows twice, you yourself will disown me three times.

Fourth Reader: Even if I had to *die* with you, I would never disown you.

Third Reader: I'm with you. Why, I would never let Jesus down. He means *everything* to me. I certainly am glad I'm not like *other* people.

First Reader: He was despised and rejected by men, a man of sorrows, familiar with suffering. Like one from whom men hide their faces, he was despised, and we esteemed him not.

Second Reader: Many have forsaken our Lord. Many have become a part of the crucifixion. Why blame the Jews or the Romans?

Third Reader: Well, *someone* certainly was at fault. That man Jesus was innocent. I'm certainly glad for their sake that I wasn't there. I would have fought with my sword to protect Jesus.

First Reader: Then the Jews began to argue sharply among themselves, "How can this man give us his flesh to eat?"

Second Reader: This is a hard teaching. Who can accept it?

Third Reader: I can! Hey, I can! I mean, after all, what would the church be without Holy Communion? That's what all that flesh business it all about, isn't it? I mean, really — I can accept it.

Jesus: This is why I told you that no one can come to me unless the Father has enabled him.

First Reader: From this time many of his disciples turned back and no longer followed him.

Second Reader: Well, they had good reason, I guess. They were confused. The teachings of Jesus aren't easy to understand. What is all this about dying to the self so you can have eternal life? It doesn't make sense sometimes.

Third Reader: I understand it. When you follow Jesus you have to die to things like self-righteousness. I don't have that problem, but I have heard that others do. I would never, *never* leave Jesus. Not *me!*

Jesus: You do not want to leave too, do you?

First Reader: Lord, to whom shall we go? You have the words of eternal life.

Second Reader: We believe and know that you are the Holy One of God.

Fourth Reader: Surely he took up our infirmities and carried our sorrows, yet we considered him stricken by God, smitten by him, and afflicted.

Third Reader: I'm glad he did. What would Easter Sunday be without the crucifixion first? Anyone ought to understand that. It's simple. I'm certainly happy to be a Christian.

First Reader: He was oppressed and afflicted, yet he did not open his mouth; he was led like a lamb to the slaughter, and as a sheep before her shearers is silent, so he did not open his mouth.

Second Reader: By oppression and judgment he was taken away. And who can speak of his descendants?

Third Reader: Wait a minute! Wait one minute! I'm one of his descendants. I follow him and don't you forget it. I'm in church almost every Sunday. I would never, *never* forsake Jesus.

On the Cross

First Reader: Yet it was the LORD'S will to crush him and cause him to suffer, and though the LORD makes his life a guilt offering, he will see his offspring and prolong his days, and the will of the LORD will prosper in his hand.

Jesus: My God, my God, why have you forsaken me? Why are you so far from saving me, so far from the words of my groaning?

Fourth Reader: Now wait just one minute. What does all this mean? Did Jesus really say that God had deserted him? How could God have deserted his Son?

Third Reader: That's simple. You see, God had to pull away from him so that he could die. There's nothing to that. It's really clear when you think about it. I see it immediately. You see, Jesus was God and God can't die. Therefore God had to leave him.

Fourth Reader: No. I don't see at all. It appears to me that if God would leave Jesus, if he would abandon him then he would abandon *us* as well. I'm confused.

Jesus: O my God, I cry out by day, but you do not answer, by night, and am not silent.

Third Reader: Oh, I forgot to tell you. He's only quoting Psalm 22. I almost forgot that. He's not really scared or hurt. It's like a show. He had to pretend to die. Well, now, that's not exactly right. He really died, but it didn't really hurt or *something* like that.

Jesus: But I am a worm and not a man, scorned by men and despised by the people. All who see me mock me; they hurl insults, shaking their heads: "He trusts in the LORD; let the LORD rescue him. Let him deliver him, since he delights in him."

Third Reader: You know he could have called down angels. Jesus didn't have to die. He wanted to die. He knew how special some of us are who follow him. He knew that some of us would never betray him.

Fourth Reader: Do you mean that you are an even stronger Christian than the apostle Peter?

Third Reader: Well, no. But Peter had his reasons I guess. All I know is that I would never have betrayed Jesus, nor helped nail him on the cross. No, not me. I'm too good a Christian for that.

Fourth Reader: Sounds like you've already reached perfection.

Third Reader: Close enough. The rest I have to get in heaven.

Jesus: Many bulls surround me; strong bulls of Bashan encircle me. Roaring lions tearing their prey open their mouths wide against me. I am poured out like water and all my bones are out of joint. My heart has turned to wax; it has melted away within me. My strength is dried up like a potsherd, and my tongue sticks to the roof of my mouth; you lay me in the dust of death. Dogs have surrounded me; a band of evil men has encircled me, they have pierced my hands and my feet. I can count all my bones; people stare and gloat over me. They divide my garments among them and cast lots for my clothing.

First Reader: After the suffering of his soul, he will see the light of life and be satisfied; by his knowledge my righteous servant will justify many and he will bear their iniquities.

Second Reader: Therefore I will give him a portion among the great, and he will divide the spoils with the strong, because he poured out his life unto death, and is numbered with the transgressors. For he bore the sin of many, and made intercession for the transgressors.

Fourth Reader: I think I'm beginning to understand what Good Friday was all about. He died so that he could make intercession for me. He died so that I could be forgiven and live a new life free of guilt. But I guess some of it will always be a mystery. Maybe we're not supposed to understand everything. Maybe we are only to accept it and be grateful.

Third Reader: I understand it. But those guys who killed him are really going to get it come judgment day. I'm sure glad that I would never do anything like that.

Jesus: I am thirsty.

First Reader: A jar of wine vinegar was there, so they soaked a sponge in it, put the sponge on a stalk of hyssop plant, and lifted it to Jesus' lips.

Jesus: It is finished.

First Reader: With that, he bowed his head and gave up his spirit.

Second Reader: The centurion, seeing what had happened, praised God and said, "Surely this was a righteous man."

Fourth Reader: When all the people who had gathered to witness this sight saw what took place, they beat their breasts and went away.

First Reader: But all those who knew him, including the women who had followed him from Galilee, stood at a distance, watching these things.

Third Reader: I would not have stood off at any distance. I would have been right in there with Jesus. Why I . . .

Fourth Reader: Why don't you shut up?

Jesus: Father, forgive them for they know not what they do.

[Note: This reading is based on Isaiah 53, Psalm 22, and the passion narratives in Saint Mark, Saint Luke and Saint John.]

Father, Into Thy Hands

A Good Friday Meditation
Luke 23:44-49

Jack Benny was once given an award and he responded in the following words: "I don't deserve this award. On the other hand, I have arthritis and I don't deserve that either."

It is difficult for us to imagine that we have enough value in God's sight that he would allow his Son to die for us on a cross. Jesus did that so that we might have eternal life. We may not feel that we deserve such a gift, but this gift has been given to us. You and I then can be gracious receivers and accept this very precious gift.

The atoning death of Jesus, accomplished for our sins, is a gift. It is not a payment for anything we did or can do. When we consider once more on this Good Friday what the Cross has meant, we can draw fresh lessons for our lives. This passage from Luke teaches us two lessons: self-denial and trust.

Self-denial means that God has given us a renewed insight as to who we are and what it really means to be called by the name "Christian." Who we are has to do with our free acceptance of Christian maturity. The more we mature into this insight, the more we become identified with the will of God and the less we worry about ourselves. It is a strange fact that once we forget ourselves truly we find ourselves.

Self-denial does not mean that we put ourselves down, but rather that the Christ on the Cross has already pulled us up. Like the thief on the cross, we are all saved only by the skin of our teeth at the last minute. The saving grace of Christ has snatched us from the jaws of death and despair.

When we look at the notion of trust we are reminded of a childhood prayer. It goes like this:

Now I lay me down to sleep.
I pray the Lord my soul to keep.
If I should die before I wake,
I pray the Lord my soul to take.

This is a profound prayer and most of us have known it since our childhood. We do not need to read any more books on prayer if only we have truly understood what this one simple prayer means.

This prayer teaches us basic trust in God. It is hard for many of us to admit that most of the anxiety we experience in this life stems really from one thing only: lack of trust in God. As we learn to trust God we allow ourselves to say with Jesus, "Father, into thy hands." Even with this last phrase of Jesus we are being taught. We are being taught trust.

For those of us who are beginners at trust we can practice a brief exercise. Right now, as you listen to these words, close your eyes. Take three slow, deep breaths. Consider for a moment the pew that is holding up your body. Feel how firm it is and how supported you feel. There is no danger of you falling because the pew will hold you up. Feel supported and trusting. Now consider the air around your face. Relax and simply feel the freshness of the air around you. Feel the relaxing quality of this free air. Notice that you breathe automatically. You do not have to think about each breath. You can trust your lungs to breathe for you. God made those lungs. Now be quiet with me for a moment and let us simply be still together. *(Pause a few moments.)*

Now gently open your eyes. Look around you and see that God was in charge of things while you had your eyes closed. You and I do not need to worry about every little thing. All we need to do, really, is relax and entrust all these matters to God. Trust starts with small steps. We practice trust in little things, like our breathing, almost without ever thinking about it. We can go on automatic pilot and let God be God.

There is an old legend that has often been told. The angel Gabriel met Christ when the Lord returned to heaven. "How did it go on earth?" Gabriel inquired. "Not so well," Christ answered, shaking his head sadly. "Mind telling me what you did?" Gabriel asked. "Of course not," Jesus responded. "I taught, I healed, and I loved. I also called twelve men to be my disciples."

Jesus and Gabriel discussed the twelve men for a time. None of these twelve seemed outstanding. They were ordinary people, much like thousands of other people living on earth. Each one of them had character traits that made them different from each other. There was Philip, who was known for his desire to know the truth. Peter and Andrew, who had been fishermen by trade, were practical men. John appreciated beauty, and Simon was the most politically conscious. Then there was Matthew with his experience and moderate amount of wealth. It was true that each was individual, but rather ordinary.

"What makes you think that you can depend upon them?" Gabriel asked, thinking that the prospects didn't look too promising. "I taught them," Jesus answered. "They are my disciples and I'm depending upon them." "And if they fail?" Gabriel asked. Christ shook his head slowly. "I have no other plans. If they fail, my mission on earth also fails."

We need to see that trust goes both ways. You and I can trust God. But can he trust us? Thank God that the twelve were trustworthy. They were able to deny themselves and be trusted. And, each of the twelve, in his own particular way, trusted God. Because of this we are here today in this church on this Good Friday.

Planning for an Easter Vigil

Every year in the congregation where I serve we have an Easter Vigil from 6:00 p.m on Saturday until 8:00 a.m. on Easter morning. It concludes with the Easter breakfast. Recently we had an open Communion where people could come and go and take Communion before breakfast. In both the Easter Vigil and the open Communion we attempt to provide space in which one can be alone with God.

We are most fortunate in that we have a small chapel in addition to the main sanctuary. But the sanctuary could be used for a Vigil. Or, a small classroom could be set aside for this purpose. For those who are homebound or afraid to go out at night, we enable them to hold their portion of the Vigil at home. We generally have a sign-up sheet with twenty-minute prayer "slots." This way a much broader segment of the congregation is involved in the Vigil.

In the chapel we place some reading material such as *Upper Room* and the Bible. However, the emphasis is upon prayer, not reading. For the last two years I have written a meditation to be used as a beginning for prayer. It provides a structure for praying. It does not dictate the content for prayer. Following is the one I used this year. If it is not useful in your situation, perhaps it will suggest ideas for one of your own. The people simply read the meditation and pray at the suggested pauses.

Easter Vigil Meditation

Have you ever waited for something that seemed would never come? As we wait this night upon the joyous Resurrection Day of our Lord Jesus Christ, let us not jump toward this dawn too quickly. Realize that abandoned feeling, that alone feeling as one feels the power of death approaching. Suffer along with our Lord and realize the words of Psalm 22. Please read this Psalm now . . .

Pray now for guidance . . . for faith . . . for thankfulness of God's love for you, so much so that he would die . . . for forgiveness of your sins . . . for your family . . . for your church . . . for its leaders . . . for your pastor . . . for your community . . . for your state . . . for your country . . . for the world to find peace . . . for the sick whom you know . . . for the grieving . . . for the lonely . . . for widows and widowers . . . for the increase of the Gospel . . . for . . . *(here add your own petitions)*. Now you might close by adding other prayers, the Lord's Prayer and by reading Mark, chapter 16.

Before you leave this place of prayer, be silent yet a few more moments and allow the Risen Christ to address you personally with his plan for you. You need only be silent and listen to your heart, for he speaks down inside you. He speaks not with noisy words, but in a voice that is like a gentle breeze. That is God's way.

Know that you are forgiven, for you have asked forgiveness. You are led by Christ inasmuch as you only let go and trust him. He will be with you always not only this day, but for all eternity. That is a long time.

Praise God this one special night by all you think, intend and do. Receive his blessing and return now to your home, a changed being with renewed power for living the faith you so often profess. Amen

Invocation for Easter Sunday

O Lord, we thank you for the Resurrection, that symbol of everlasting life. May we share that life with Christ which is beyond decay and death. Like the stone that was rolled away, our sins have been rolled away. We proclaim the hope of Easter, and, inasmuch as we can, live in your Kingdom even now. We know that we are not of the world, but while we are in the world we trust ourselves to your care. Allow us not to look back at the empty tombs of our lives, but to the future we all have in Jesus Christ. Destroy the traitor and resurrect the saint in us. This is our prayer. Amen

The Resurrection of Our Lord

An Order of Worship

Prelude and Lighting of Candles
Symbolism of Christ as the Light of the World.

Litany of Praise
(Loudly and joyfully from the back of the sanctuary)

First Voice: Praise the LORD.
Second Voice: Praise God in his sanctuary; praise him in his mighty heavens.
Third Voice: Praise him for his acts of power; praise him for his surpassing greatness.
First Voice: Praise him with the sounding of the trumpet, praise him with the harp and lyre,
Second Voice: Praise him with tambourine and dancing, praise him with the strings and flute,
Third Voice: Praise him with the clash of cymbals, praise him with resounding cymbals.
Choir: Let everything that has breath praise the LORD.
People: Praise the Lord!

Invocation: Heavenly Father, we do indeed praise you this day with all that is in us. Our very beings shout with joy because we remember the victory won over Satan by your Son Jesus. Father, we remember that the grave could not hold him. We believe what is written, that he arose this day. Re-create in us today the power of Easter Day and equip us with that power that we may overcome discouragements and fight on for the faith. Amen

Hymn: "Christ the Lord is Risen Today"

Dramatic Skit by Children (or Selection by Children's Choir)

First Reading: Isaiah 25:6-9

Choral Anthem or Handbell Choir Selection

Minister: Then Peter began to speak: "I now realize how true it is that God does not show favoritism but accepts men from every nation who fear him and do what is right.
People: **You know the message God sent to the people of Israel, telling the Good News of peace through Jesus Christ, who is Lord of all.**
Choir: You know what has happened throughout Judea, beginning in Galilee after the baptism that John preached —
Minister: How God anointed Jesus of Nazareth with the Holy Spirit and power, and how he went around doing good and healing all who were under the power of the devil, because God was with him.
People: **We are witnesses of everything he did in the country of the Jews and in Jerusalem. They killed him by hanging him on a tree,**
Choir: But God raised him from the dead on the third day and caused him to be seen.
Minister: He was not seen by all the people, but by witnesses whom God had already chosen —
People: **By us who ate and drank with him after he rose from the dead.**
Choir: He commanded us to preach to the people and to testify that he is the one whom God appointed as judge of the living and the dead.
People: **All the prophets testify about him that everyone who believes in him receives forgiveness of sins through his name.**

Hymn: "He Lives" (or: "Crown Him With Many Crowns")

The Holy Gospel: John 20:1-18

The Sermon

Baptism of new Christians, Reception of new members, Confirmation

Nicene Creed

Offertory Service
Offertory Statement   Pastor
Special Music
Doxology

Litany of Consecration
Liturgist: You have given us eternal life.
People: We offer you, in humility, these gifts of money.
Liturgist: You have given us eternal life.
People: We offer you ourselves.
Liturgist: You have given us eternal life.
People: We offer you our service.

Silent Prayer

Pastoral Prayer and Prayer for the Sick

Lord's Prayer *(said by all)*

Closing Hymn: "Because He Lives"
                  (or: "Lord Jesus, I Love Thee")

Extinguishing the Candles
Taking the Light from the Altar into the World.

Choral Benediction

Postlude

The Easter Church

A Sermon for the Resurrection of Our Lord
John 20:1-18

I know you have heard of Easter eggs and Easter bunnies. Perhaps also you know about Easter bonnets and Easter dresses. But have you ever considered an Easter *church*? An Easter church is more than a place where we come wearing new print dresses or blue suits on a very special day of the year. An Easter church lifts up a special symbol to the world around it. It lifts up an empty tomb and says: "Look! He is risen!"

An Easter church is a place of refuge for those who feel forsaken. It is a field of victory for those who strive and find that Christ gives them the power to go on and to keep their heads turned up toward heaven. The Easter church is the workroom where the product of eternal life is made. An Easter church schools us in God's ways and teaches us his laws. It proclaims joy and faith and coaxes from us all that is divine and good in us.

An Easter church needs an Easter preacher. It should be one chosen by God to proclaim the Resurrection message to a burdened world. An Easter preacher is not an employee of the local congregation, but rather stands as a witness of the Resurrection by his or her ministry. An Easter preacher is a faithful servant who preaches God's Word and not simply intellectual concepts that the preacher has discovered.

An Easter preacher proclaims an Easter sermon that brings comfort, that awakens us to repent and to remind us of the victory over sin. An Easter sermon pulls out the faith that people have had all along, even when they felt weak. An Easter sermon should challenge people to grow and become all that God wants them to become. Easter sermons should inspire, but should also lead us to repentance and guide us toward grace.

I hope that you can say this church is an Easter church. Church is a special covenant that God has given us to bind us to one another. Bonhoeffer once said: "It is easily forgotten that the fellowship of Christian brethren is a gift of grace, a gift of the kingdom of God that any day may be taken from us, that the time that still separates us from utter loneliness may be brief indeed. Therefore, let him who until now has had the privilege of living a common Christian life with other Christians praise God's grace from the bottom of his heart. Let him thank God on his knees and declare: It is grace, nothing but grace, that we are allowed to live in community with Christian brethren." (Bonhoeffer, *Life Together*)

The Easter church is a gift of God. It allows us to experience love and acceptance. It reconciles us to ourselves and to our neighbors. It guides us to heaven when it faithfully preaches the Bible. To paraphrase Karl Rahner, something happened at the tomb which we hope to have happen here and now in our own local Easter church.

You and I can look forward in faith to being resurrected like our Lord and King was that first Easter. The Easter church allows us to experience the power of Resurrection in our lives here and now. But the final, absolute resurrection will only occur with the Second Coming of Jesus Christ.

Our Easter church exists only by the grace of God. We must not forget this. The Easter church stands as a watchtower that sends out a beacon, a searchlight that looks for the lost. Anyone who is hurting can look to Christ, and the best way Christ can be seen is in the church and its members. You and I are the Easter church.

Our Easter church must realize that it only exists to be of service to God and others. We are challenged to go and make disciples. We are in church not only to be fed, but to be provisioned for ministry. This is our first and only real reason for existing as a church.

Let us recall that first Easter for a moment. We are told that when Jesus first appeared to Mary after the Resurrection, she did not recognize him. There are two main factors here that are of interest to us in today's Easter church:

1. She could not recognize him because of her tears. They blinded her eyes so that she could not see. When we lose a dear one, there is always sorrow in our hearts and tears in our eyes. It is natural, when sorrow comes, that we cry as did Mary. But we should never let our pain blind us to the glory of following Jesus Christ. Tears there must be, but through these tears we still catch a glimpse of the glory land.

2. Mary could not recognize Jesus because she insisted on facing the wrong direction. She could not take her eyes off the tomb. As a result, she had her back to him. She supposed that the one speaking to her was only the gardener. It is often so with us. At a time of grief and pain our eyes are upon the cold earth. We must lift our eyes toward heaven.

Our loved ones who have passed away are not in the tomb. They are already living with God in some mysterious way. We must never let our tears blind us to that fact. Alan Walker, in "Everybody's Calvary," tells of officiating at a funeral for people to whom the service was only a form to go through. These had neither Christian faith nor Christian connection.

He writes, "When the service was over a young woman looked into the grave, and said brokenly: 'Good-bye, father.' It is the end for those who have no Christian hope."

But for the Christian it is not good-bye. It is, "Until we meet again!" This is what Jesus was saying to Mary. He was saying, "Nice to see you again, Mary. Why are you crying? Didn't your faith tell you that death could not be the end for the Son of God?" And Jesus has not only addressed Mary in this way. He speaks so to us as well.

What, then, does an Easter church teach? What does an Easter preacher preach? Very simply that Jesus overcame the grave and those who believe in him will do so as well. Perhaps we have a hard time hearing how marvelous that is because we have heard it so often. Realize that you are not going to stay dead! That is the incredible message of the Easter church.

Charles Templeton once wrote, "What a difference the resurrection makes! Look at the scene on Friday and all you see is failure. But look again on Sunday and all is changed. Christ has taken the Cross and, using it as a battering-ram, has driven the end of the sepulcher to let in the light of an eternal day. The grave has become a gateway. Death is now a door.

"The tombstone has become a milestone and the graveyard has become a brighter place, festooned about with hope. Christ, the Divine Samson, has picked up the iron gates of impossibility and has carried them off. What a difference the resurrection makes. What a difference in the life of Mary and the disciples. What a difference in the history of the world."

Let us close with a medieval legend that speaks of the power of Easter and what an Easter church is really all about. It can remind us that our task is really to witness to others that heaven shall soon be our home. What joy that will be!

Brother Thomas went out through the gates of his monastery to gather firewood in the forest. As he was gathering his twigs, a bird on a branch over his head began to sing a beautiful song. The song was glorious and Brother Thomas put down his gathered wood and listened, enchanted.

Finally the bird finished its song and flew away. The monk picked up his wood again and started back to the monastery. When he rang the bell at the gate one of the other monks appeared, but did not recognize Brother Thomas. Brother Thomas told the gatekeeper that he had only left a half hour ago to gather firewood.

The gatekeeper said, "We have no Brother Thomas in this monastery. But wait. I will call one of the older monks." Soon a venerable old monk appeared.

The old monk said, "I don't know you. I never saw you.

But I do now remember that one of the old monks told me, when I came here as a young monk, that there was a Brother Thomas who once went out to gather faggots, and never returned. But that was a hundred years ago."

Brother Thomas had listened to the beautiful music not for one half hour. One hundred years had passed, so sweet was its song! Such will be the joys of heaven. And this is the message of the Easter church. We know a secret that we would like to share with the whole world. Death is a cruel joke played by Satan. There is nothing to fear if we keep our eyes on Jesus. The Easter church proclaims joyfully that he is risen!

Appendix

Hymns for Lent

Amazing Grace
What Wondrous Love Is This
Out Of the Depths I Cry To Thee
When I Survey the Wondrous Cross
I Need Thee Every Hour
What a Friend We Have In Jesus
Just As I Am
Pass Me Not, O Gentle Savior
Brightly Beams Our Father's Mercy
Have Thine Own Way, Lord
Rescue the Perishing
Rock Of Ages

Are Ye Able?
Beneath the Cross Of Jesus
Where He Leads Me
Wonderful Grace Of Jesus
Jesus, Lover Of My Soul
Revive Us Again
Be Not Dismayed
How Great Thou Art
I'll Go Where You Want Me To Go
It Is No Secret
Just a Closer Walk With Thee
Sweet Hour Of Prayer

Hymns for Holy Week and Easter

Because He Lives
Christ Arose
Christ the Lord Is Risen Today
He Lives
I Serve a Risen Savior
Low In the Grave
Were You There?
All Glory, Laud And Honor
On A Hill Far Away
The Old Rugged Cross
There Is A Fountain Filled With
　Blood
And Can It Be?
Jesus, Keep Me Near the Cross
Jesus Paid It All
O Sacred Head

What Wondrous Love
Worthy the Lamb
All Hail the Power
Come, Thou Almighty King
Holy, Holy, Holy
Joyful, Joyful
O Worship the King
Sometimes "Alleluia"
Alas! And Did My Savior Bleed
In the Cross Of Christ I Glory
Must Jesus Bear the Cross Alone
O Love Divine, That Stooped To
　Share
Take Time To Be Holy
'Tis Midnight, And On Olive's Brow
Praise the Lord Who Reigns Above

About the Author

Gary Houston has been a member of the North Indiana Conference of the United Methodist Church since 1980. Prior to that he taught Philosophy and World Religions at Ball State University. He has taught at Christian Theological Seminary, Indiana University at Kokomo, and at The School of Theology, the University of the South.

Seven of his books have been published. They fall into the following divisions: two in Tibetan Studies, two on Christian-Buddhist Dialogue (editor), and three (sermon collections) for C.S.S. Publishing Company. He has written and published over a dozen articles and fifty book reviews on various subjects. He is a frequent contributor to *Emphasis, a Preaching Journal for the Parish Pastor,* and has published sermons with Seabury Press and JLJ Publishing.

His hobbies include computering, languages, and music. His wife Joyce puts up with it all.

www.ingramcontent.com/pod-product-compliance
Lightning Source LLC
Chambersburg PA
CBHW060858050426
42453CB00008B/1009